MW01048149

To:

How to **Overcome Every Obstacle . . .**and Land on Top

By Patrice Lee

Copyright 2011
First printing: June, 2011
Second printing: August, 2011
Third printing: June, 2012
2nd and 3rd Edition: March, 2013, Oct., 2014

Published by Leep4Joy Books, a Division of
Feinstein Development & Associates
Printed in the United States of America

Library of Congress Catalog-in-Publication Data

Copyright Registration: #
ISBN -13: 978-1477508275

Edited by: Mary Edwards
          Leaves of Gold Consulting, LLC and
          Stephen A. Moore
Cover Art: Bob Ivory, Jr.,
          Ivory Coast Media

Send all correspondence to: Leep4Joy Books, a
division of Feinstein Development and
Associates, P.O. Box 48172, Oak Park, MI 48237

How to Overcome Every Obstacle
. . . and Land on Top
Table of Contents:

How to Overcome Every Obstacle

Preface

Though we are living in one of the greatest periods in history, we are also enduring some of the toughest economic conditions. This book was written for those who choose to live life above the circumstances, regardless of how things may look to the natural eye.

You may be facing some of the toughest times of your life right now; but did you know you can get through it if you just put your mind to it? I want to assure you, ***you can,*** and ***you will overcome***.

I am pleased to share with you some techniques that will yield effective results. If you are willing to make a few adjustments to your daily routine, ***you will overcome*** every trouble.

Let's take a journey through the next few pages and find out how. :)

How to Overcome Every Obstacle

"It's in the Attitude"

*One person, with determination, can change the environment around him. But in order to change the conditions of the world, **we**, collectively, must change our hearts, our mindsets, and our attitudes. When **we** change, together, **we can** change the world.*

How to Overcome Every Obstacle

What I Mean Is . . . .

Let's define some key words as they are used in this book, so that our understanding is the same.

"Clutter" – things or people that take up space or time in your life that have no purpose; people or things that add no value to your life.

"Negativity" – implied negatives; words, deeds, or people that become your obstacle; an obstruction to something good.

"Obstacle"- something that affects your life in a negative way; someone or thing that impedes progress; a negative force in your life; anything negative; a strong opposition to a positive outcome. Adversity, trouble, circumstance, or concern may be used congruently with "obstacle."

"Overcome"–to rise above the problem or situation.

"Toxic" – damaging; unhealthy.

"Recovering from all the Negativity. . . In Your Life"

Everyone has to deal with adversity at some point in their life. Even good people experience tough times. Some individuals are confronted with obstacles or negative encounters more frequently than others.

How do you handle adversity? How we choose to handle the bully at school, job loss and financial hardship, a troubled marriage, long-term illness, broken relationships, or the loss of a loved one, will affect us and those we communicate with either positively or negatively.

What is your approach to handling money matters, when you know that resources are limited and you've depleted the budget before all of the bills are paid?

Can you bounce back after a broken relationship with a determination to mend, forgive, and improve poor communication in the future?   How do you manage stress at work?

Can you go back to school with your head held high after being taunted or teased the day before?

How would you respond, if you discovered that you've burned the main dish just minutes before your dinner guests arrived?

Ask yourself:
Do I allow yesterday's problem to affect today's actions/reactions?   Am I able to "let go, forgive, and release" on a daily basis without the aftermath of anger, despair or unnecessary grief?

Sometimes one negative comment or circumstance can have the same damaging effects on a person's emotions as that of the strong and deliberate attack of a Linebacker's blind side tackle.

Did you know that dwelling on one negative thought, or spoken word, can throw you off course for an entire day, even longer, if you don't reject it and replace each negative encounter with something positive?

The average person may need to hear as many as four (4) positive statements to erase the affect of one (1) negative statement.

That is why it is important to rise above the impact of every negative word, conversation, circumstance or thought as quickly as possible, in order to experience and enjoy the maximum benefits of a balanced and fruitful life.

Quick recovery is important because the negative impact from one negative word, phrase or inflection:

1. Can have an immediate effect on your feelings and emotions

2. Will affect your reactions to others

3. Will slow down your response time

4. Will give you a distorted view of the world and yourself

5. Can affect you physically and/or mentally over time.

Removing the negative influences will bring positive changes to your life. Anything in your life that is not a positive force is considered to be a negative force. In order for your life to flow in the most positive fashion, you will have to remove all negative influences.

If it isn't helping you, strengthening you, enhancing your gifts, bringing increase to your life, causing you to be fruitful, and complementing you in every way, you need to let it go.

Once you've removed the negative influences, you will be able to change the direction of your thoughts and how you've been thinking; and ultimately the direction of your life. The thing that remains constant for all of us is that we have a choice. We can control how and what we think about.

"As a man thinketh in his heart, so is he." In other words, whatever you continue to think about is what you will have, and all that you continue to rehearse (practice) is what you will become.

It's up to you to choose how you will spend your day, whether it's happy or sad, in victory or defeat, content, or at peace.

"Forgive. Release! Let It Go!!!"

Forgive. Release! Let it go!
Who cares how long it's been? It's time to grow. Your hurt and shame stand in the way of each new day.

Forgive. Release! Let it go!
Opportunity is here if you'll open the door,
With a healthy attitude and a determined mind, To help you endure the test of time.

Forgive. Release! Let it go!
Dare to be bold, courageous, and strong.
Plunge in with confidence,
In God put your trust.

Forgive. Release! Let it go!
It's time to live and your time to grow.
You deserve to be happy, to let your spirit be free.

Be free from the hurt, the guilt and shame.
Be free to be you and live again. Be free to
Forgive. Release and let go!!

<u>Thought</u>:

Your willingness to forgive in any circumstance, will take you beyond hurt and allow healing to take place. With pure forgiveness comes a change in attitude; and a positive atmosphere is automatically created.

Quick Recovery Requires:

Changing Your Mindset

If you change how you think, you can recover from any negative thought, word, deed or habit.

Pure Happiness

Sometimes adversity comes because of self-indulgence, and because you like the way a substance makes you feel. It could be prescription drugs, alcohol or a combination of the two of them. Prescribed medication is used to conceal both physical and emotional pain. Alcohol is by choice; but both can be addictive.

Both, prescription drugs and alcohol can take the brain from a productive state to a non-productive state, causing your judgment to be impaired. While they alter your ability to reason, excessive amounts can also alter your lifestyle, causing you to become co-dependent.

Life is so much more enjoyable and carefree when you realize how happy you can be without them. In fact, you can be happy and productive at the same time. You can remain in that happy state, by monitoring what you allow to enter into, or take up residence (stay) in your mind.

Eight Steps to Follow:

Whenever you experience adversity from the impact of a negative word, or deed, of which you were the focal point, or if you're facing major setbacks in your life because of an obstruction in your path, follow these **eight (8) principles:**

You must:

1. **Cast Out Every Negative Thought.**

   Replace those negative thoughts with every positive affirmation that you believe for yourself, or desire to have, that oppose the negative words directed toward you. Say out loud every positive statement associated with your belief.

   If you must acknowledge the effect it had on you, or how it made you feel, do so quickly, and move on. And remember that this too shall pass.

a. Think pleasant thoughts.

Many times it helps to do something pleasant, such as listen to your favorite music, read a great book, or look at a funny movie; attend a concert, see a great comedy, or go for a nice walk. Engaging in any one of these activities listed can help change or redirect your thoughts, but reading an encouraging chapter/verse from God's Word will refresh your spirit.

So often, people in cold climates complain about the winter weather, particularly the snow and frigid temperatures, which last a total of 3 or 4 months maximum, in most changing climates. If they would concentrate instead on a new hobby, develop their creative side, or spend some time serving others—help a senior citizen, become a volunteer for youth, etc., the winter season would pass more quickly.

Have you ever observed a seasonal tree in winter? A seasonal tree is one that changes with the seasons. These trees, like bears, go dormant during the winter.

Yet, seasonal trees are very much alive during the winter months, despite their striking appearance of lifelessness. In fact, they are full of life and thriving abundantly on the inside.

Just as the tree lives on through the winter months, you can think of negative words and deeds as your winter season. As you go through your winter elements of adversity, great opposition, and the many roadblocks or obstructions of life, it becomes necessary to visualize spring coming.

b. Look beyond the current set of circumstances.

In other words, you have to look beyond winter to get to the pleasantries of spring--fresh rain, beautiful flowers, and prepare for summer--picnics on beautiful green grass, and lovely landscapes, etc.

In order to do this, you must learn to smile from the inside out. As you practice smiling on the inside, it will begin to reflect in your outward appearance.

Have you ever thought about the person (in a coma) who can't feel anything at all? What about the man or woman that can't speak, who is unable to verbalize/express how he/she feels (about anything)?

Since you can do absolutely nothing about the weather anyway, why complain at all? Move your thoughts forward to the next season, think "spring," and think "May flowers."

Get in touch with nature; just a little bit of contact goes a long way. As you look toward the next season, you will see that change is constant; and change is consistent.

C. It's going to happen anyway

Have you ever noticed that regardless of what the weatherman predicts, and whether the groundhog sees his shadow or not, that the trees still bud in early March, the days continue to get longer, and the sun just seems a little brighter each day.

So, the next time you feel the urge to complain about the weather, acknowledge the conditions, but consider the positives. You might say: "It's cold, but spring is coming. We got seven (7) inches of snow yesterday, but I'm looking forward to those May flowers."

When you become more thankful for all of the good things that have occurred in your life, you will find less time for complaints. It's o.k. to acknowledge the hurt and/or disappointment, but also acknowledge the good things that happen in your life.

By becoming more thankful, even for the little things, you will have and enjoy more positive outcomes.

2. **Release the Poison.** And release quickly.

   All poison is toxic. Toxic wastes must be eliminated or destroyed carefully. As in the destruction of toxic wastes, there must be a release of those poisonous, negative words, phrases or statements through verbal expression.

   Unreleased feelings of anger, hurt or pain can harm us mentally, physically or emotionally, and can eventually lead to further damage internally. In order to avoid internal damage, these feelings should be released with open communication by talking to a counselor, family member or close friend.

   So you must push past the pain and the hurt. You must continue to push past the disappointment and the dirt (things that people may have said). Just keep pushing until you've been made whole again.

The faster you release the hurt from a painful experience, the shorter the healing process, the less damage to your emotions, etc. When you're faced with adversity, you can increase your endurance level by making a decision to push past the pain.

Maybe there has been a time at your workplace when your supervisor, who may have been having a bad day, would speak in a negative tone of voice for no apparent reason. Naturally, some feelings of anger may surface, but there's no time to be upset because that work on your desk still needs to be done.

Your decision to swallow your pride, be the bigger person, and remain positive can work in your favor. When you're striving to be the best, there's absolutely no time to sulk, no time to be angry. Besides, great minds don't make excuses, waddle in the mud, or throw in the towel. Great minds keep dreams alive.

The lesson to be learned here is that it doesn't matter if a person you encounter is having a bad day. It's important that you not allow anyone to influence the flavor of your day in a negative way.

Just keep a good attitude and maintain a positive state of mind at all times. Even when you are challenged on every side, and your back is against the wall, you must envision yourself free from the entanglement and focus on the bigger picture.

With the right attitude, there's no mountain too high, no valley too low, no dream too far to reach. If you stretch your faith, and focus on all the positives, you can attain any goal.

Talk to God about everything, great and small. Seek His guidance.

Acquire His wisdom before you start anything new. Trust Him. He cares about you.   God never fails.

3. Have a Moment of Reflection.

Know that it's o.k. to have a moment of reflection; to reexamine who you are, and how you came to be that wonderful person that you are.

I immediately become thankful for my parents, for teaching me to have integrity and to respect others, by their example. I am grateful for whom I am, and who I have become, because of it.

What are the contributing factors that have made you the great person that you are? Who spoke those life-changing words to you at a time when you needed it most?

Who gave you a hand when you felt yourself slipping on a downward slope? Who smiled at you when your world was spinning 'round? Who picked you up as you were falling to the ground?

Who exonerated you and kept you lifted with exhortation? Who replaced strong persecution with positive communication? Who is the one that cared the most, when you just couldn't see past the frustration caused by purposely intended exploitation?

Perhaps there is an individual who has made a difference in your life; a person who has been a positive role model, or someone that said (these words), "I believe in you," and affirming, "You can do it," at a time when you most needed to hear it.

Yes, there is a reason that you are here, well-adjusted, and mended, with minimal scar tissue, minus a tear or two. For this you have much to be grateful. A note of thanks you should give, as you reflect on how wonderful a life you have actually lived.

Reflect and be thankful. Reflect; look ahead. Keep moving forward, and continue to give thanks.

4. Seek Peace. Find Peace Within.

When adversity comes, the best thing you can do is remain calm. To handle adversity without stress would require placing your trust in a loving God.

God is bigger than your problem, and He promises peace in the midst of the storm. Trust Him to work it out.

<u>Peace is incredible</u>. When you find peace, embrace it. Let nothing come between you and that wonderful peaceful feeling. This is where you belong. This is where you must stay in order to achieve your heart's desires, dreams, and aspirations.

Learn to love yourself. One way to love one's self is through positive affirmation. Give yourself a smile every day. Meditate on good thoughts. Think about all the great things that have happened in your life continuously. Reflect on your achievements and all the things you have accomplished in life.

Creative juices and thoughts will begin to burst on the inside; and in your most peaceful state is where your creativity will come alive. There will be an air of expectancy and excitement as you allow the creative juices to flow.

Think about those things that make you happy. Imagine yourself surrounded by those things daily. Concentrate on your goals, and purpose to fulfill those dreams that you have. As you expound on them, those once hidden talents and gifts will be revealed (unveiled).

You will find that peace is incredible.

5. Simplify Your Life.

Still working on that peaceful feeling we just talked about? What's keeping you from having a peaceful life? Do you have a peace-blocker?

Is your life clutter-free? Are you hoarding things that you don't need, will never use? Or are there people in your life that shouldn't be? Clutter can cause a state of unrest.

If you're experiencing conflict or being bullied on Facebook / Twitter, find a new pastime. Close the account(s) and make new friends. Love yourself; and show love and kindness to those you meet.

Clutter drains your energy, impedes progress, and keeps you from having clarity of thought to achieve your dreams. Remove the clutter from your life, physically (people, things, and all the unnecessary stuff), spiritually, mentally, and emotionally.

Clearing your head of past fears and disappointments will make room for creative thinking and innovative ideas. Become more selective in every area of your life, especially your friends, thoughts, actions and hobbies. Exercise discipline. Simplify your life.

Can we address the "shopaholic" for a moment? If you're a shopaholic, you have to learn how to toss things out to avoid becoming a hoarder. : (

You are a hoarder, if you look in the closet and find shoes there so old that they curl up at the toes from age--even worse--if they don't fit any more because the fabric has decomposed. (lol) Toss them out!!

Clutter is an ugly vein in your life. Get rid of it. If you really want to simplify your life, toss out at least one or two items for each new item purchased. Can you stop shopping for the things you don't need until you've tossed out all the things not needed and not being used?

Would it help you to know, that until I made up my mind to refresh every room, and clean out every closet, basement storage areas too, clutter remained an obstacle for me? The real breakthrough was getting started.

I always felt that 1) I could not do this task alone, because I was sentimental. 2) I never knew where to begin, because organization was not my strong point, and I thought you had to be organized to get started. 3) I was simply afraid of the task.

Well, I am so glad I did because I have been tossing, cleaning, organizing, and donating ever since, and I can't stop. It's both rewarding and invigorating. And the house looks and feels better.

To the passive hoarder, who continually adds items to car trunks/back seats, month after month and promises to clean it out as soon as the weather breaks: "Hhmmm. Which season are you waiting for?"

I have seen things get so out of control that only the driver could fit into his five (5) passenger seat vehicle. Maybe today would be a good day to unload. No more excuses. Let's get started. :)

Take time to set some goals. Then have a plan for how you will execute your goals. Set realistic time lines.

Hint: Work can be fun when there's a little competition. Find someone else who needs to do the same thing and see who can finish first. Do something to celebrate the winner.

6. Listen to the Music.

Are you listening to the music of life? Have you ever noticed the designs in printed fabrics? Sometimes they are geometric shapes and sometimes abstracts. The one thing they have in common is that their patterns are repeated over and over again.

Just as in beautiful tapestry, patterns repeat themselves. So too, in life, are many beautiful patterns and rhythms. History, like the patterned fabric, repeats itself. From one year to the next, from decade to decade, there is repetition. You can see it in nature, in families, culture, fashion trends and politics.

If you lost your job, just know there's a better one coming. Don't stop looking. If you were cheated in a business venture, learn from your mistakes. Don't give up. Be wiser the next time. Forgive.

Tune in to the rhythm of life. Let it be music to your ears. If you tune in, and observe carefully, you may be able to avoid some common pitfalls by learning from the mistakes others have made.

It's so much better to learn from someone else's mistake than to experience the trouble yourself.

7. Surround Yourself With the Right People.

These are the individuals who will love and accept you for who you are. They will always allow you to be true to self, the ones who allow "you," to "just be you" everyday of the week. :)

Hard to find people like this? And it may take a while, but they're out there. Trust me; it is well worth the wait, until you find each other.

There is no greater support on earth than people supporting, lifting up, pumping up, and motivating one another for a good cause. We really do need each other.

Sometimes one outstretched hand of encouragement can make all the difference in the world. We must unselfishly do the same for others.

It's refreshing; in fact, it's invigorating to speak kind words

41

and do kind deeds for others. And the more you do it, the happier you'll be.

The world can be a much better place, if we all work together to make it so. Together, let's raise the altitude of our minds, and raise our level of thinking. It will be positively reflected in our attitude(s) towards others.

8. Make Minor Adjustments Daily.

You can overcome every negative word, thought, deed and action, and "land on top," when you learn to smile from the inside out. As you practice smiling on the inside, it will be reflected in your outward appearance.

I have listed 26 minor adjustments to help you develop your smile on the inside. These adjustments, if practiced daily, will make a positive difference in your life.

They are:
  a. Expect everyday to be a great day.
  b. Smile, from the inside out. Wear it every day.
  c. Laugh often. LOL every day.
  d. Be thankful for the little things.
  e. Be kind to yourself.
  f. Pray always. Forgive others instantly.
  g. Never go to bed angry.

h. Show kindness to others. Do something nice just because. . .
i. Walk in love.
j. Enjoy the simple things in life.
k. Read (and meditate) the Word of God daily.
l. Refresh your thoughts constantly.
m. Keep busy; refuse to have idle time.
n. Accept change without compromising your own values.
o. Volunteer happily.
p. Encourage others.
q. Practice discipline as a routine.
r. Be a problem solver.
s. Stand tall.
t. Let God know how special He is. Give Him praise.
u. Make a difference in the world.
v. Improve yourself. Become less critical of others.
w. Find ten things to be thankful for every day.
x. Keep a song in your heart.

y. Be inspired. Pursue your dreams.

z. Be happy, just being you.

Practicing any combination of these minor adjustments daily will yield a happy, more productive life. The happier you are, the healthier you will become; for a merry heart doeth good like a medicine. Happiness will even be reflected in your smile.

How to Overcome Every Obstacle

How Do I Land On Top?

From the title, H*ow to Overcome Every Obstacle . . . and Land on Top,* you might ask, "How do I . . . land on top?" Give the problem to God, and think on things that are lovely and of a good report. As you lean on Him, God will fill you with His peace.

Sometimes you may have to go through a valley before you can appreciate the peace that only God can give. His peace can take you to the mountain top and keep you there.

Seek and find peace of mind and spirit. Let God's peace sustain you. **His mountain top peace is all you need.**

As you experience peace on a regular basis, you'll find that you have more time to simply enjoy life, concentrate on your goals, and see your dreams manifest. The things that you have worked so hard to achieve will seem to unfold before you and become a reality.

"No dreamer is ever too small; no dream is ever too big." Anonymous

A Thought to Remember:

"It's Always about the Attitude"

Don't let the storms of life overwhelm
you.
Never let the obstacles get in your way.
For if you continue to rise above the
circumstances,
You can embrace the positive changes of
each new day.

How to Overcome Every Obstacle

"You Can Overcome Too"

There was a period of time when I was incapacitated because of a foot injury. I was in a cast for four months. I remember enduring much pain for an extended length of time.

Unfortunately, I had complications. I experienced greater pain once the cast was removed, and had difficulty maneuvering from point "A" to point "B." On top of that, I received a negative report from several doctors about an underlying condition affecting the healing process. They said there was nothing else they could do for me.

I could have chosen not to walk because of the pain, or taken medication for it. But I chose to push past the pain. I refused to give up. I asked God to heal me and He did. I walk today, without assistance, and without pain.

"Heal me, O Lord, and I shall be healed; . . ."
Jeremiah 17:14a

Applying God's Word to your situation yields results. Speak the Word only, and believe.

You can overcome **job loss** if you:

- Update your resume
- Search the job market for new opportunities
- Prepare for the interview
- Be flexible
- Think and remain positive
- Believe in yourself
- Know your strengths & weaknesses
- Know that there is a job for you
- Consider creating one; become your own boss.

If you're facing **financial hardship:**

- Seek wise counsel
- Downsize your spending
- Get on a budget and stick to it
- Find organizations that will work with you to conquer the problem of debt
- Begin saving a percentage of dollars earned per pay period
- Be disciplined; waste not.

Special note to those experiencing financial hardship:

Many people have been affected by the current "economic crisis." Some are using it as their excuse for money problems, when their financial crisis may have been self-imposed.

Is it fair to blame the economy for everything that's gone wrong in your financial world, when your financial troubles could be from a poor decision you made months, even years ago?

Sometimes one wrong decision can turn your life upside down. And sometimes the recovery period from that wrong decision can take years. Learn to move forward and learn to save and spend less.

For **illness** or medical emergency:

- Have faith in God; remain prayerful
- Rest often
- Be supportive of one another; work as a team.
- Keep family close.

If you have experienced the **loss of a loved one:**

- Lean on, trust, and rely on God
- Let His comfort sustain you
- Take time to regroup; . . .vacation
- Don't spend too much time alone.
- Family support is crucial.

Mending **broken relationships:**

- Forgive; be the first to apologize
- Be honest; admit your faults
- Know when to walk away and not look back (counseling suggested)
- Grow; learn from your experience.

You can **conquer the bully** if you:

- Ignore him/her (if possible)
- Keep your distance
- Replace fear with faith
- Travel in multiples, not alone
- Seek wise counsel
- Hold your head high. . . and know that everything is going to be alright.
- (Children) Talk to your parents
- (Parents) Listen to your children

Special note to the bully victim:

So, somebody's talkin' about you, and it's not true? *Ignore it!* You're not accepted in their circle of friends? *It doesn't matter.* They don't like the clothes you wear? *So what!*

If someone has hurt, embarrassed or humiliated you in any way, report it immediately. It is imperative that you keep your parent(s) informed about each incident every time you are attacked. Talk it out. Forgive that person(s). And keep talking until you feel better. Replace the pain of humiliation with positive thoughts and activities.

If you were bullied on the way to school, consider carpooling, or take a different route. Try to surround yourself, when possible, with people who have your best interest at heart.

You have a purpose for being here; and you must find out what your purpose is. Your life has special meaning to your family members and closest friends, because there is only one you.

Be selective with whom and what you give your time, attention and talents to. Keep your thoughts elevated above the chatter (frivolous conversations) to avoid being distracted.

Continue to weed out the distractions by focusing on your dreams and aspirations, and set goals. Keep looking up. Don't look back. Keep moving forward, and soar like an eagle!

Remember to:
Practice the 8 steps outlined in this book. The more you practice each step, the faster the obstacles in your life will seem to dissipate and go away.

You are an "overcomer."

You don't have to wait until the storm is over to make a difference in the world; because if you're waiting for a perfect time, it may never come. Work through the storm, until you see the sun again.

They Overcame Great Obstacles

The following great men and women overcame tremendous obstacles in their young lives to achieve outstanding accomplishments, set records, make scientific discoveries, create, invent and compose.

How to Overcome Every Obstacle

Lucille Ball

Lucille Ball overcame tremendous rejection as she pursued her passion for acting, to become one of the most popular and influential stars in America during her lifetime. She went on to receive accolades for having one of Hollywood's longest careers, especially on TV.

"Lucy," as she was called, was born in Jamestown, New York, on August 6, 1911. Her mother became a young widow before Lucy's 4th birthday. Her father's death altered their lives drastically.

With her heart set on becoming an actress at age 15, Lucy quit high school to attend the Anderson School for the Dramatic Arts of New York. After completing only two weeks of training, Ms. Ball was told she "had no future at all as a performer."

But with extreme determination, Lucy overcame being fired from several

Broadway productions, a crippling illness, and other disappointments to become a comedienne, film, television, stage and radio actress, model, executive producer and star of many sitcoms, including "I Love Lucy" and more.

So thankful that Lucille Ball never gave up on acting, for we would have missed out on this legend of comedy.

Ludwig van Beethoven

He overcame an abusive childhood and deafness to become an extremely gifted composer of classical music and one of the most respected musicians in the world.

Ludwig van Beethoven was born in Bonn, Germany on December 16, 1770 and was the first of three children born to Johann and Maria van Beethoven and to survive infancy. There were two other siblings out of seven that also lived.

The grandson of the musical director and the son of a tenor singer, who also taught piano and violin, Ludwig became a child prodigy and eventually studied under Austrian composer Joseph Haydn as a young adult.

Ludwig's Dad wanted to make his son a child prodigy, like Mozart, but a lack of organizational skills and his alcoholism prevented him from accomplishing his desire for his son.

As a young child under his Dad's tutelage, if young Ludwig played the wrong chord or hit the wrong key his father might slap, shove, or punch him, and sometimes even lock him in the basement (cellar).

Young Beethoven gave his first public piano performance at seven and published his first work at twelve.

In 1796, Beethoven was at the height of his musical career, when he began to lose his hearing. The hearing loss was a result of a severe form of tinnitus. And in 1809, Beethoven resolved to composing music because he could no longer hear himself play. He continued to compose until his death, almost 40 years later, some of the most beautiful music that is still performed today.

Some of his most beautiful symphonies composed, symphony #3–8, were composed after his severe hearing impairment. One of the greatest classical pieces Beethoven composed was his "Fifth Symphony."

Beethoven believed that music was more than mere entertainment, but that it also had a moral and humanistic value, and that music would help us emerge.

Christy Brown

Irish author, painter and poet, Christy Brown, learned to paint and write with the only muscle he could control; his left foot.

Born June 5, 1932, in Crumlin, Dublin, Ireland, Christy, was one of 13 surviving children (out of 21) born to Bridget and Paddy Brown. He was diagnosed with severe cerebral palsy at birth.

Cerebral palsy denied Christy control over speech and physical movement. His mother always encouraged him to overcome his disorder by talking to him. At age five, young Christy gained considerable control over his left foot inspiring his mother to teach him the alphabet. He learned to spell, and eventually, to read.

Christy Brown overcame his paralysis to become celebrated around the world for his artistic ability. He is most famous for his autobiography: "My Left Foot."

How to Overcome Every Obstacle

Dr. George Washington Carver

Although his early life was filled with poverty, cruelty, and prejudice, he became scientist extraordinaire, man of faith, humanitarian and respected pianist.

Raised by his mother's former slave owners, Moses and Susan Carver, George Washington Carver was born into slavery on July 12, 1864, in Diamond Grove, Missouri. Young Carver was separated from his mother during infancy, and remained frail through childhood.

Unable to attend school before age 12, and denied admission to universities because of his race, Carver continued to pursue education and excelled in the fields of science and art.

The first Black to serve on the faculty at Iowa Agricultural College in 1894, Carver received his Master's Degree in 1896, and accepted the invitation to serve as Director of Agriculture at Tuskegee Institute. It was there that he began to soar in the field of science.

Upon accepting a position at Tuskegee, he realized that he had found his purpose in life: His desire to help former the slave population become efficient in farming became his passion. And here he found happiness and honor in being helpful to the world. While at Tuskegee, Dr. Carver encouraged farmers to rotate their crops in order to preserve the nutrients in the soil.

In collaboration with Henry Ford he developed alternative fuel from soybeans and perfected the process of extracting rubber from the milk of the golden rod plant. He remained committed and once raised money for Tuskegee Institute by touring as a pianist.

He was so devoted to his work there that he turned down a $100,000.00/year position from Thomas Edison.

During his tenure at Tuskegee, Dr. Carver discovered over 300 products from the peanut alone, including peanut butter, ink, shampoo and facial cream; 150 products from the sweet potato, and more than 75 products from the pecan.

Dr. Carver was invited to speak to the U. S. Congress and received numerous consultation requests from others.

Bessie Coleman

Denied the opportunity to pursue her dream of flying in her native land, Bessie Coleman overcame strong racial barriers to become the first black woman in the world to own an aviator's license, and the first black female to own an international pilot's license.

Elizabeth "Bessie" Coleman was the tenth of thirteen children born to sharecroppers, George (a Cherokee) and Susan (a Black woman) Coleman, in Atlanta, TX, a town of a 1,000 people, known for fortunes made on railroads, oil and lumber.

Little Bessie became fascinated with airplanes at a young age. But, in 1901, when her dad decided to relocate the family for a second time due to racial barriers, her mother decided not to go, and at nine, young Bessie became keeper of the house while her mom went to work.

Bessie was an outstanding math student. When she wasn't working the cotton fields or caring for four younger siblings, she'd walk four miles to an all-black, one room schoolhouse to learn more math. At twelve, Bessie completed the eighth grade and became hungry for more knowledge.

It took six years to save enough money from her laundry job to go to school. In 1910, she enrolled at the university in Langston, OK, but exhausted her savings in one term.

Still infatuated with the airplane, Ms. Coleman applied to flying schools in the United States; but was denied entry. She taught herself French, and in November, 1920, sailed across the Atlantic Ocean to Le Croy, France to achieve her dream.

Bessie obtained her pilot's license in seven months from Federation Aeronautique Internationale in 1921, and flew in her first air show on September 3, 1922, at Glenn Curtis Field in Garden City, NY. She dazzled audiences everywhere she went with her "barrel-roll" and "loop-the-loop" stunts, proving that neither race nor gender can stop you from achieving and exceeding your goals.

Inducted into the Texas Aviation Hall of Fame, in 2000; Chicago, declared May 2nd as Bessie Coleman Day, and streets and schools have been named in her honor.

Thomas Alva Edison

Dubbed the father of the light bulb, the phonograph and motion picture, Edison had received more than 400 patents by the age of 40. Perhaps the greatest obstacles he had to overcome was deafness, for he was 80% deaf in his left ear and completely deaf in the right ear.

Born on February 11, 1847, and raised in Port Huron, MI, Thomas A. Edison eventually overcame being labeled at school for his inability to concentrate, and being partially deaf, to become an American inventor – most recognized for the light bulb, scientist, and businessman.

Young Thomas was extremely inquisitive. As a young child, he asked "why" to almost any statement that was made and when he finally started school at age eight, his curious nature left the teacher extremely irritated. Rescued from that one-room schoolhouse - which held 38 other students - after only 12 weeks of school, his mom decided it would be in Thomas' best interest to home school him instead.

Mrs. Edison did everything she could to

quench his thirst for knowledge, but Thomas' thirst for knowledge remained throughout life. He studied or read every book he could get his hands on and practically devoured the World Dictionary of Science by the time he was 12.

Despite the negative words of his teacher who said he was too stupid to learn anything, and being fired from his first two jobs for being "non-productive," Edison developed many devices that greatly influenced life around the world.

After many great inventions, Edison experienced many failures too, including concrete furniture, homes made out of cement, and the talking doll. But he refused to stop trying.

As an inventor, Edison made more a 1,000 (unsuccessful) attempts before inventing the light bulb. And when a reporter asked, "How did it feel to fail 1,000 times?" He replied, "I didn't fail 1,000 times; the light bulb was an invention with 1,000 steps."

Thomas Edison had many great inventions, with his positive attitude and great sense of humor, earning his last patent - # 1,093 at 83.

Regina Engelhardt

Regina Engelhardt, is a world reknown artist-of all mediums-from pencil to paints, oils to restorative art, a sculptor, and cosmetologist. She was born October 1, 1928. Ms. Engelhardt shared this moment in history in her own words: "I remember World War II, when Stalin and Hitler invaded Poland, as if it were yesterday.

The country was divided. Our family, who lived in the eastern part of Poland, landed under Russian occupation for two years.

When soldiers entered our territory – everything - the store and banks closed. People helped one another by sharing what they had, creating "beaut-i-ful things" out of scraps. We were scheduled to be taken to Siberia.

After Hitler invaded Russia, we came under German occupation. This was the beginning of the revolution. The Ukranian bandits killed everyone who was not Ukranian. And we were in the middle of it all.

As Hitler was losing the war with Russia, he took people with him to be sold as slaves, into forced labor. We had only an hour notice before we were to leave our home, to live in the camp, surviving on a bowl of soup and a piece of bread each day, if there was no shortage.

We remained apart from our parents and family until the war was over; and gathering the remnants we had left, made our new home in the U.S. Some of us, as a result of the physical conditions, torturing, and cruel deaths witnessed of our loved ones, remained in a state of shock for many years.

With prayer, a positive approach, and a sense of humor we overcame every hardship, for these challenges we face in our lives bring a greater understanding of ourselves, and a oneness with others. We realize that we need one another. It helps us to grow spiritually. It causes us to become more inventive, caring and compassionate."

Ms. Engelhardt's art is displayed at the National Museum of Women in the Arts, Washington, D.C. and Althorp, England. She has won many awards at the local, national and international level.

Michael J. Jordan

Born February 17, 1963, in Brooklyn, NY, and raised in Wilmington, North Carolina, Michael Jordan loved sports, and played baseball, football, and basketball competitively.

Michael Jordan initially tried out for the high school basketball team but was turned away more than once. The high school varsity coach finally told Jordan that he was too short to play basketball, and tried to convince him to consider another sport, during his sophomore year.

Determined to prove his worth, Jordan became the star of Laney High's junior varsity squad, scoring several 40 point games that year. The following summer he grew four inches and trained rigorously. Thus, the basketball star was born.

Jordan was recruited by the Chicago Bulls in 1984, prior to completing his degree. He quickly emerged as a league favorite, entertaining crowds with his prolific scoring.

His leaping ability, earned him the nicknames "Air Jordan" and "His Airness." He was dubbed the "greatest basketball player of all time" by the National Basketball Association.

Helen Keller

Born June 27, 1880, in Tuscumbia, AL, Helen Keller was a bright infant, interested in everything around her. She was struck with an illness which left her deaf, blind and mute before her second birthday. Although she was labeled as a wild, destructive child, she displayed strong signs of intelligence.

Helen had little communication with the rest of the world, until she met a very special teacher, Anne Sullivan, at age six. Within 30 days of their first meeting, Helen was learning as many as 30 words per day. Helen mastered Braille, learned to write, and how to use a typewriter by the age of 10.

By age 16, she could speak well enough to attend preparatory school and college. She raised funds for organizations, spoke in over 25 countries and brought hope to many people. Ms. Keller overcame many obstacles in her own life and dedicated her time and gave of her service to improve the lives of others.

How to Overcome Every Obstacle

Dr. Benjamin E. Mays

He was the youngest of eight, born August 1, 1894, in South Carolina, just two decades after slavery, Benjamin E. Mays used every opportunity, including a spirit of excellence and higher education to improve his quality of life.

His outstanding leadership and service as teacher, preacher, mentor, scholar, author and activist in the civil rights movement influenced and redirected the lives of many, including Andrew Young and Dr. Martin Luther King.

Although, he attended school only four months a year, Mays' graduated as Valedictorian in 1916, overcoming poverty, racial discrimination, and his Dad's protest against education.

His accomplished included the following: 1920 - Received B.A., Bates College in Maine, and graduated Phi Beta Kappa 1922 - Became an ordained minister; pastored Shiloh Baptist Church of Atlanta. 1925 – Earned M.A. degree from the University of Chicago

1926 - Appointed Executive Secretary of the Tampa, Florida Urban League
1928 - Became National Student Secretary of the YMCA
1934 - Accepted Dean of the School of Religion position at Howard University
1935 - received a PhD in Ethics and Christian Theology

Mays joined the faculty at Morehouse College to teach math, psychology, and religious education and served as debate coach in 1921. Despite all that he accomplished, he was not allowed to vote until 1945, at 51 years old.

Upon retiring from Morehouse, Dr. Mays was elected President of Atlanta Public School Board, orchestrating it's peaceful desegregation. Every Tuesday morning, Dr. Mays challenged and inspired his students to excellence in scholarship and in life. "The sky is your platform," he said. "You've got to reach for the moon."

"It must be borne in mind that the tragedy of life does not lie in not reaching your goals; the tragedy lies in not having any goals to reach."

Mma. Agnes Chenngwe Mazile

Mma Agnes Chenngwe Mazile, the fifth of six children born to Chiliwa and Senkgabe Mbaakanyi on March 19, 1932, in Serowe, was one of the greatest farmers ever to till the Botswana soil. Mmagae, as she was affectionately called, was a prominent businesswoman, respected community leader and passionate farmer. She and her husband, Phenyamere M. Mazile, operated several stores in Serowe for many years.

From a young age she learned how to drive a tractor and heavy duty truck(s), for which she was later licensed to operate. In this male dominated role, she faced many challenges, but she overcame them all.

Mma Mazile's incredible work ethic kept her working from 6a.m. to 6p.m daily. She seldom took time to rest. She raised cattle, including bulls, and flocks of sheep.

She farmed and packaged sorghum, millet and samp under the brand Naswi. She also grew beans and maize, and continued to lead the team of 30 employees, while managing more than 100 hectares of farm land, upon her husband's death. One cannot imagine all of the obstacles she had to overcome.

Returning from one of her marketing trips (fruits and vegetables) to South Africa, she became fascinated by the processes she observed on a dairy farm. Mma Mazile thought, "I can do that." And she enjoyed such success with dairy that her farm – Naswi Makoro Farm - became a major supplier of milk, and one of the top five in Botswana, supplying dairy to retail outlets, government institutions such as the Botswana Defence Force (Paje), schools, hospitals and prisons.

Naswi Makoro Farm was used as an educational training facility, allowing for observations, demonstrations and for mentoring. Mma Mazile hosted many government activities on her farm, including World Food Day. She received the prestigious presidential award for meritorious service for her work.

Mma Mazile left an indelible impression upon the lives of those she encountered daily, and was a tower of strength to those that knew her. In her words: "The only thing that keeps me going is work" and "gagona kgomo ya boroko," which means "you can't sleep all day and expect to prosper."

She had four children: A son-farmer/mechanic, 3 daughter's-PhD/Ed (one Ambassador to the U.S.)

President Franklin Delano Roosevelt

Born January 30, 1882, in Hyde Park, New York, Franklin D. Roosevelt attended both Harvard University and Columbia Law School. His display of courage and strength should be a reminder to all that a disablement in one area of life should not handicap you in another.

Stricken with poliomyelitis at age 39, Franklin Roosevelt continued to pursue life with passion, vigor and extreme courage. He was elected Governor of New York in 1928, seven years after being diagnosed with polio.

Just four years later, Roosevelt was elected to the office of President of the United States. He was so popular that he was reelected three times. The Social Security Act of 1935, for working Americans, was passed during his presidency. Retirees still enjoy these benefits today.

Polio did not stop Franklin D. Roosevelt from attaining his goals in life. In words spoken at his Inaugural Address, he said, "The only thing we have to fear is fear itself."

Edith Spurlock Sampson

Successful lawyer, judge, debater, and advocate for social justice, Edith Spurlock Sampson, was the first woman to earn a Master of Laws from Loyola University (1927); the first African-American delegate to the United Nations; elected the first Black woman judge in United States history (1962); and the first Black U.S. representative to NATO.

One of eight children born to Louis and Elizabeth Spurlock, in Pittsburg, PA on October 13, 1898, Edith Spurlock left school at 14 for a full-time job cleaning and de-boning fish. Sampson once told Reader's Digest, "I suppose we were poor, but we never knew it. We wore hand-me-down clothes, and we all worked. Her family worked hard, owned its own home, attended church, and obeyed the law.

Enduring many financial hardships, she returned to school, graduated from Peabody High and worked her way through college. She graduated from the New York School of Social Work and became a Chicago social worker by day, and a John Marshall Law School student at night.

Edith Spurlock overcame many hurdles to accomplish many first and succeed in life:

1924 – Opened a law office, South Side
1925 – Earned her Jurist Doctorate Degree
1927 – Earned a Master of Laws from
      Loyola Univ. Graduate Law School
1927 – Passed the Illinois Bar exam
1934 –Practiced before the Supreme Court
1947 –Appointed Assistant State's Attorney
      in Cook County Illinois
1949 – Chosen to represent Americans on
      the Round-the-World Town Meeting
1950 – U.S. delegate to the United Nations,
      appointed by President Truman
1961 – 1962 Appointed to serve on the U.S.
      Citizens Commission for NATO
1962 – Elected associate Judge of
      Municipal Court, Chicago, IL
1966–1978 Assoc. Judge for Circuit Ct.

Edith Spurlock-Sampson rose from poverty to become the first black attorney, judge, and UN delegate, to practice law before the U.S. Supreme Court, opening doors and paving the way for all women.

Madame C. J. Walker

Born the fifth of six children to slave parents, Owen and Minerva Breedlove, Sarah was the first child born into freedom, on December 23, 1867, in Delta, LA. Both parents died, leaving her an orphan at age seven. She and a younger sister were left to fend for themselves, as they learned to survive many hardships. Sarah married at age 14. And at 18, she gave birth to her daughter, Lelia. She became a widow at 20.

Like many women of her era, Sarah experienced hair loss. Because most Americans lacked indoor plumbing, central heating and electricity, they bathed and washed their hair infrequently. She experimented with home remedies and products already on the market until she developed her own shampoo and ointment.

Through the introduction of "The Walker System," she revolutionized black hair care by developing new products and a grooming system for black hair. In 1906, Madame Walker toured the country, promoting her products, lecturing and empowering her agents, while her daughter Lelia ran the mail order system from Denver, Colorado.

From 1908 - 1910, she operated a beauty training school in Pittsburg, PA. And in 1910, Madame C. J. Walker moved her office headquarters to Indianapolis, IN, where she had access to eight major railway systems. By 1919, the C. J. Walker Manufacturing Company, of Indianapolis, IN, employed and had trained a sales force of more than 3,000 men and women throughout the U.S., Costa Rica, Panama, Cuba, Jamaica and Haiti.

She became a neighbor to John D. Rockefeller, with the completion of her newly constructed home in Irvington-on-Hudson, New York, in August, 1918, and died shortly after on May 25, 1919, at 51.

Madame C. J. Walker overcame incredible odds to become the wealthiest woman in America, and was "America's first female self-made millionaire." Walker used her prominent position to oppose racial discrimination, and her massive wealth to support civic, educational and social institutions to assist African-Americans.

What If . . . ?

Can you imagine **what** course these great men and women's lives' would have taken **if** they had pondered over any one of the negative circumstances they were facing?

They chose not to feel sorry for themselves. These great men and women chose not to have a pity party. They chose instead to persevere. They did not give up; but overcame every obstacle to achieve greatness.

Although these men and women experienced great success in life, their achievements are not to be compared to the one who made the greatest provision for mankind; when God sent His only Son, Jesus Christ, to sacrifice His life for every man, woman, boy and girl to have the choice of eternal life. And because of the debt He paid through His death, burial and resurrection, you can live a life of peace and have victory over every obstacle too.

How to Overcome Every Obstacle

The Greatest Provision for Man
"JESUS"

He was born in a manger and wrapped in swaddling clothes at birth. He lived a very humble life; and, in His youth, chose carpentry as His field of work. His name is Jesus.

This man, Jesus, is full of compassion, love and mercy, and always concerned about the needs of others. While on earth, He served others and demonstrated unconditional love as He served.

Jesus, the King of kings, experienced rejection, betrayal, and the extreme discomfort of ridicule and mockery throughout His life on earth. These were the sacrifices He made for mankind.

Jesus came to earth for the sole purpose of redeeming man from a life of sin and shame. But He, who was sinless, had to bare our sin and accept our pain through the stripes He received on the cross, that the world might be saved through His death, and receive the gift of eternal life.

Jesus took a beating for us. He shed His blood for us. He was bruised for our iniquities. They thrust a crown of many thorns upon His head for us. He was nailed to the cross. They pierced His side.

He came to bring healing to the nations, to give eternal life to a lost and dying world. Jesus made the ultimate sacrifice for you and me when He died on the cross.

Life offers us many troubles, but God wants to heal and mend the broken-hearted, restore marriages and families.

> *"For God so loved the world, that He gave His only begotten Son, that whosoever believeth in Him should not perish, but have everlasting life"* (John 3:16).

> *"That if thou shalt confess with thy mouth the Lord Jesus, and shalt believe in thine heart that God hath*

raised Him from the dead, thou shalt be saved" (Romans 10:9).

"If we confess our sins, He is faithful and just to forgive us our sins, and to cleanse us from all unrighteousness" (1 John 1:9).

If you've been contemplating the best time to accept Jesus into your heart, now is the time to receive Him as Lord of your life. Today! Invite Jesus in.

Let Him have the spot where clutter used to be. Give Him full reign (in your life). Draw close to Him and experience God's perfect peace. His peace will make you happy on the inside.

The ideal time to establish yourself in Christ is while everything is going well with your body, mind, and spirit. During this period, you can study and meditate on God's Word, pray and give thanks, as you worship Him and build up your faith without a motive (need, desire).

Spending quality time with Him gives you strength, increases your faith and causes you to have great joy. With increased faith, you can believe God for what may seem impossible (to man), even through the most difficult seasons of your life.

You must never give up. Always believe, remain hopeful, and have faith. :) Talk to God about everything, because He really cares about you.

~

To receive Jesus as Lord of your life, say this prayer out loud: *"Dear Heavenly Father, I believe you sent your only Son, Jesus to earth that I might be saved, and that He died on the cross and arose on the third day. Today, I invite you to come into my heart Lord Jesus, and save me now. I repent of my sins and ask that you cleanse me from all unrighteousness in Jesus' Name. Amen."*

The angels in heaven rejoice each time this prayer is prayed out loud. That is how special you are to God. He loves you so, so much.

Inner Peace: There's Nothing Like It

With inner peace:

--you can have a cheerful disposition, even when it looks like there's no hope.

--you won't complain about your troubles; but give thanks for the expected outcome.

--you can be happy just being you.

--you can receive criticism without resentment.

--you can conquer tension and go to sleep without medication.

--you can relax and not be stressed.

You may go through many valleys in life; but God will keep you in perfect peace, if you keep your mind stayed (focused) on Him. (Isaiah 26:3)   Let God renew (refresh) your mind continually.

"In all thy ways acknowledge Him, and He shall direct thy paths" (Proverbs 3:6).

"And the peace of God, which passeth all understanding, shall keep your hearts and

minds through Christ Jesus. Finally, brethren, whatsoever things are true, whatsoever things are honest, whatsoever things are just, whatsoever things are pure, whatsoever things are lovely, whatsoever things are of good report; if there be any virtue, and if there be any praise, think on these things" (Philippians 4:7, 8).

Sometimes you can guard yourself from the negative information--world news, local news, breaking news, the weather, special reports, and a household repairman's assessment. Sometimes you can't. Sometimes you have to turn off the noise, step back, close the door, and get away from it all. And sometimes you just have to draw nigh to God and pray, and not be affected by all the noise.

Protecting Your Spirit from the Pressures of Life

Maybe you've experienced great disappointment, or maybe the pressures of life seem almost impossible for you to bear. There's good news. You can find comfort in God's Word. Finding, and applying the right scripture to your specific area of need can bring relief.

Sometimes all you need is an encouraging word or two from a friend. But, when your friends aren't there to encourage you, you may have to encourage yourself. These promising scriptures will help you do just that:

"Fear thou not; for I am with thee: be not dismayed; for I am thy God: I will strengthen thee; yea, I will help thee; yea, I will uphold thee with the right hand of my righteousness. Behold, all they that were incensed against thee shall be ashamed and confounded: they shall be as nothing; and they that strive with thee shall perish"(Isaiah 41:10-11).

Now that sounds like a powerful God to

me. One day when I was at my lowest point, I opened my Bible to those two verses in Isaiah that I'd never seen before, and knew that God was about to turn things around for me. And He gave me the strength to endure until He did. His Word, His promises changed my life.

"Fear not; I will help thee" (Isaiah 41:13b). It helps to know that God has our back. With Him on the job, fighting on your behalf, you don't need anybody else. You win!

On top of all of that, He tells you, and constantly reminds you not to fear. Why? Because fear is the opposite of faith, and in order to believe His promises, you must have faith.

"Fret not thyself because of evildoers, neither be thou envious against the workers of iniquity. For they shall soon be cut down like the grass, and wither as the green herb. Trust in the Lord, and do good; . . .Delight thyself also in the Lord: and He shall give thee the desires of thine heart. Commit thy way unto the Lord:

trust also in Him, and He shall bring it to pass" (Psalm 37:1-5).

God never wants to see you fret or shed a tear. He'll even give you the things you want, if you 1.) keep your joy, and 2.) delight (remain happy) in Him.

"Rest in the Lord, and wait patiently for Him. . .Cease from anger and forsake wrath...For evildoers shall be cut off: but those that wait upon the Lord shall inherit the earth" (Psalm 37:7-9). *"Trust in the Lord with all your heart; and lean not unto your own understanding. In all thy ways acknowledge him, and He shall direct thy paths"* (Proverbs 3:5-6). When we place total trust in Him, it automatically puts our spirit at ease-no matter what the circumstance.

"I will lift up my eyes unto the hills, from whence cometh my help. My help cometh from the Lord, which made heaven and earth" (Psalm 121:1-2). Our God promises to keep you, to preserve you, and all you have to do is look up to Him and trust Him

to do exactly what He says He's going to do. Refuse to doubt, and stay in faith.

"And the peace of God, which passeth all understanding, shall keep your hearts and minds through Christ Jesus" (Phillipians 4:7). And then, He promises to give you peace, and to keep you in perfect peace, if you'll just keep your mind and your thoughts on Him. (Look up Isaiah 26:3.)

$\sim$ Live in His peace $\sim$

Remember: You can do all things through Christ who strengthens you. ☺

Faith-Building Scriptures for Troubled Times

The Word of God says: *"If God be for us who can be against us?"* (Romans 8:31b)

<u>You can say</u>: "If God is for me, who can be against me?"

The Word of God says: *"Is anything too hard for the Lord?"* (Genesis 18:14a).

<u>You can confess</u>: "Nothing is too difficult for Thee O Lord; there's absolutely nothing too big for You to handle."

The Word of God says: *"I can do all things through Christ which strengtheneth me"* (Philippians 4:13).

<u>You can say</u>: "I can do all things through Christ who strengthens me."

The Word of God says: *"For by thee I have run through a troop: by my God have I leaped over a wall"* (2 Samuel 22:30). *And they overcame him by the blood of the Lamb, and by the word of their testimony"* (Revelation 12:11).

<u>You can confess</u>: "I am an overcomer. I have the victory through Christ."

God says: *"Ask, and it shall be given you; seek, and ye shall find; knock, and it shall be opened unto to you"* (Matthew 7:7)

"Just Ask"

Remember to:

Begin and end each day with a prayer of thanks. Acknowledge God and ask Him for guidance in all of your affairs. Trust Him to direct your paths. Stay in God's presence. For in His presence is fullness of joy.

He will keep you smiling on the inside. Just one smile can change your life. Why not give yourself the first smile every day? Then, let your smile communicate kindness and warmth to others, as you continue to smile from the inside out.

You may order additional books by going to: **amazon.com**

Patrice Le**e** continues to write and publish books. She speaks at conferences, seminars, to K-12 students, church youth groups, parents and teaching staff and organizations.

If these books have helped you in any way, please forward your comments:

Patrice@Leep4Joy.com

All scripture references are taken from the King James Version of the Holy Bible, unless specified otherwise.

Biographical information taken from the following resources:

Cyprus, Sheri. "Wisegeek," Sept, 2010.

http://www.answers.com/topic/edith-s-sampson-1

http://www.biography.com/people/ludwig-van-beethoven-9204862?page=2

http://www.biography.com/people/thomas-edison-9284349

www.biography .com

www.britannica.com

www.ideafinder.com/history/inventors/carver.htm

http://www.lkwdpl.org/wihohio/cole-bes.htm

http://www.mmegi.bw/index.php?sid=6&aid=33&dir=2009/September/Thursday24

www.Tuskegee.edu/about_us/legacy_of_fame/george_w_carver.

www.whitehouse.gov/about/presidents/franklindroosevelt

www.wikipedia.org/

About the Author:

Patrice Lee experienced bullying in the workplace, however, she entered the workplace daily with a smile, a positive attitude and a willingness to do and be her best.

She offers readers refreshing advice and practical solutions to some of life's problems. Leep4Joy Books & Resources share a message of faith, hope and love.

www. Leep4Joy. com

PatriceALee@gmail.com

Made in the USA
Charleston, SC
24 July 2015